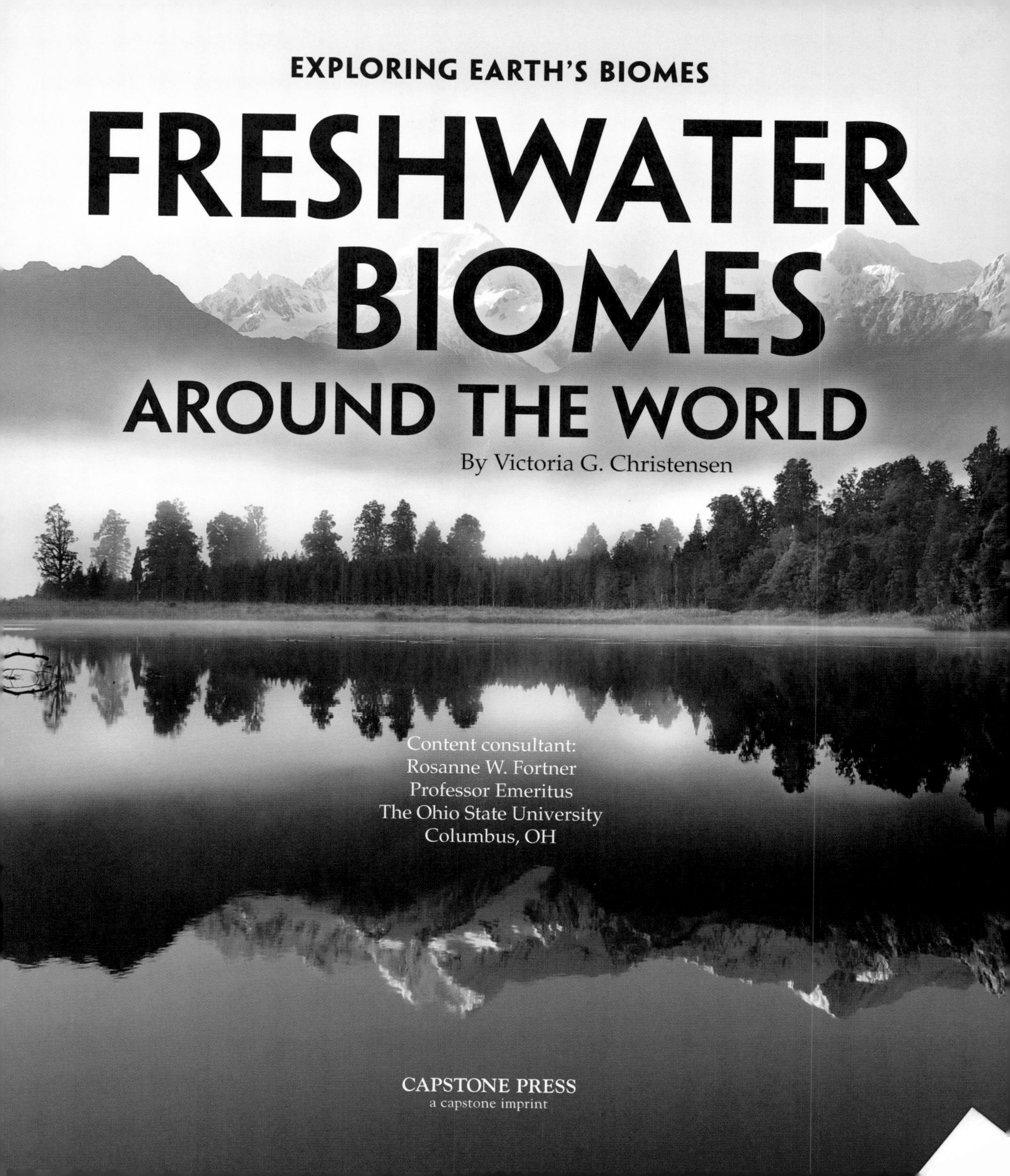

EXPLORING EARTH'S BIOMES

FRESHWATER BIOMES
AROUND THE WORLD

By Victoria G. Christensen

Content consultant:
Rosanne W. Fortner
Professor Emeritus
The Ohio State University
Columbus, OH

CAPSTONE PRESS
a capstone imprint

Fact Finders Books are published by Capstone Press
1710 Roe Crest Drive, North Mankato, Minnesota 56003
www.capstonepub.com

Library of Congress Cataloging-in-Publication Data
Names: Christensen, Victoria G., author.
Title: Freshwater Biomes Around the World / by Victoria G. Christensen.
Description: North Mankato, Minnesota: Capstone Press, [2020] | Series:
    Fact Finders. Exploring Earth's Biomes | Includes index. | Audience: Age
    8–9. | Audience: Grade 4 to 6.
Identifiers: LCCN 2019002051| ISBN 9781543572117 (hardcover) | ISBN
    9781543575330 (paperback) | ISBN 9781543572179 (ebook pdf)
Subjects: LCSH: Freshwater ecology—Juvenile literature.
Classification: LCC QH541.5.F7 C59 2020 | DDC 577.6—dc23
LC record available at https://lccn.loc.gov/2019002051

Editorial Credits
Gina Kammer, editor; Julie Peters, designer; Morgan Walters, media researcher;
Kathy McColley, production specialist

Photo Credits
Alamy: Nature and Science, top 23, Saxon Holt, 27; Science Source : Carlyn Iverson,
9, Claus Lunau, bottom 18 ; Shutterstock: Avesun, 14, Beat J Korner, 17, CLP Media,
bottom 4, Designua, 21, djgis, spread 4-5, spread 6-7, DJTaylor, bottom right 26, FedBul,
19, Huy Thoai, bottom 10, icemanphotos, spread 8-9, spread 10-11, spread 12-13,
Lillac, bottom 20, Michael Stabentheiner, top 11, Milos Kontic, (kayak) Cover, Oko Laa,
bottom 24, Rainer Lesniewski, 13, Rocksweeper, spread 14-15, spread 16-17, Sebastian_
Photography, (lake) Cover, stihii, 7, Sundry Photography, 29, SUPACHART, design
element throughout, TTstudio, spread 26-27, spread 28-29, VarnaK, spread 18-19,
spread 20-21, spread 22-23, spread 24-25; Wikimedia: Geoff Ruth, 15, USGS, 5

PRINTED AND BOUND IN THE USA.

PA70

TABLE OF CONTENTS

CHAPTER 1

WHAT IS A FRESHWATER BIOME?

Imagine hopping over a small stream. Water trickles over wet stones. You don't quite make it across and splash into the cold water. But when you try to move, you can't. Your shoes are stuck in mud. Did you know you just stepped into a freshwater biome?

FACT BOX
Only 2.5 percent of Earth's water is fresh. Of all the fresh water on Earth, about 99 percent is either underground or frozen.

Biomes are large areas that have certain types of climates, plants, and animals. The five main biomes are **aquatic**, forest, desert, grassland, and tundra.

The freshwater and marine biomes are aquatic biomes. Marine biomes are salty. Freshwater biomes have water with very little salt. The salt content in fresh water is less than 1 percent.

Where is Earth's Water?

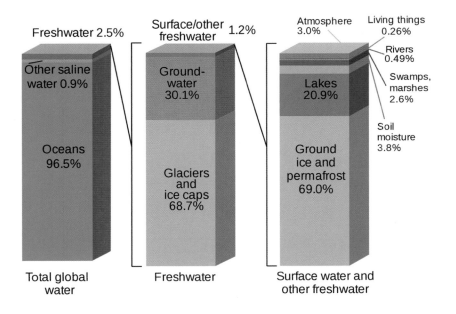

Freshwater 2.5%

Other saline water 0.9%

Oceans 96.5%

Total global water

Surface/other freshwater 1.2%

Ground-water 30.1%

Glaciers and ice caps 68.7%

Freshwater

Atmosphere 3.0%

Living things 0.26%

Rivers 0.49%

Lakes 20.9%

Swamps, marshes 2.6%

Ground ice and permafrost 69.0%

Soil moisture 3.8%

Surface water and other freshwater

Fresh water is found all over the world. Freshwater biomes include lakes, rivers, ponds, and wetlands. Wetlands are areas such as swamps or bogs that are **saturated** with water.

aquatic—having to do with water
saturated—soaked with water

5

Earth's geology and geography control where we find fresh water. The water in some places is still. In other places, it flows.

Lakes and ponds are still bodies of water. Some lakes form in basins created by the shifting of Earth's crust. Some form in craters of extinct volcanoes or meteors that hit Earth long ago. Many lakes and ponds formed from melting glaciers.

Rivers and streams are flowing water. All rivers start at a high point, called headwaters, and flow to a lower point. A river can start with a trickle of water on a mountain. It collects more water as it flows downhill. Usually, the river becomes wider. The width, direction, and speed of the river depend on the slope of the land. Rivers shape our landscape too. They can wear away the soil and rocks in a process called erosion.

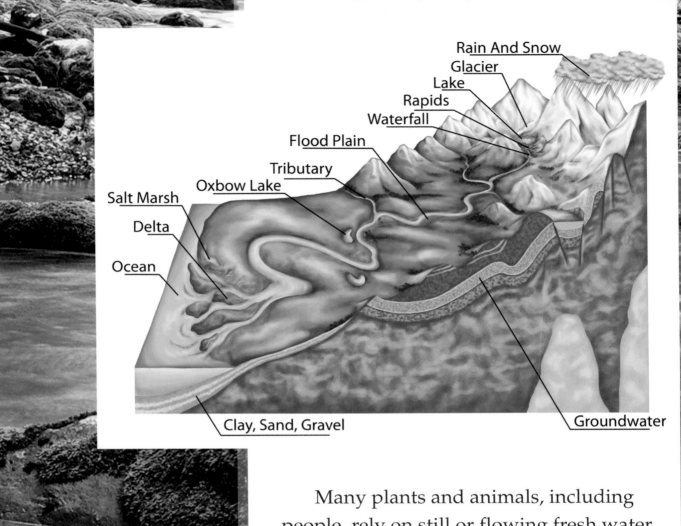

Rain And Snow
Glacier
Lake
Rapids
Waterfall
Flood Plain
Tributary
Oxbow Lake
Salt Marsh
Delta
Ocean
Clay, Sand, Gravel
Groundwater

Many plants and animals, including people, rely on still or flowing fresh water to survive. They find ways to **adapt** to freshwater biomes. Over time, groups of people have settled near sources of fresh water for drinking, fishing, washing, traveling, and watering crops. People also use fresh water to produce electricity.

adapt—to change in order to survive; a change in an animal or plant to better fit its environment is called an adaptation

CHAPTER 2

A FRESHWATER FOOD CHAIN

Some animals and plants live in the water. We call these **organisms** aquatic life. Other organisms in freshwater biomes live on land. Just like people, they need water to survive. Both aquatic and land organisms play a role in the biome.

To keep the biome healthy, plants, animals, and people work together. Energy passes through a biome in the form of a food chain. Think about a lake biome. The food chain starts with the sun shining on the lake. **Algae** in the lake use the sunlight for **photosynthesis**. This process turns the sun's energy into food. Next, **zooplankton** eat the algae. In turn, insects eat the zooplankton. Fish eat the insects. Larger animals such as eagles or bears eat the fish. People also eat fish. Every part of this food chain is important to keep the biome in balance.

algae—a simple plant without stems, leaves, or roots
organism—a living thing like a plant, animal, or cell
photosynthesis—the process of using sunlight to make oxygen and food from carbon dioxide and water
zooplankton—a small animal plankton in the water

Sun

Red-winged Blackbird

California tree frog

Great Blue Heron

Raccoon

Mosquito

Flame darner

Algae

Mosquito larvae

Water boatman

Sacramento perch

Western toad

Many food chains together form a food web. A food web shows the different paths that connect organisms to each other.

ADAPTATION

The animals and plants that live in fresh water have adapted to it. How they've adapted depends on their location in the biome. For example, some floating plants don't have roots. They have adapted to absorb water through their leaves or stems.

Water lilies are floating plants that have roots. They absorb **nutrients** through the soil at the bottom of a pond or lake. But mosses don't have roots. They live in moist and shady places, sometimes near swamps or bogs. They absorb nutrients through their tiny leaves.

water lilies

webbed duck feet

Animals living in freshwater biomes have features to help them survive. Ducks have webbed feet to paddle through water. Beavers have flat tails to help them swim. The fat that fills their tails also helps keep the beavers warm.

Many organisms have adapted to flowing water. In rivers, some plants have strong roots that keep them anchored. If they weren't anchored, the **current** might carry them away. To hold on to rocks and twigs in a fast current, some fish, such as the Hawaiian goby fish, have suction cups!

current—flowing water moving in one direction
nutrient—a substance that provides nourishment needed for growth and survival

13

WATER AS A RESOURCE

Just as animals have adapted to different places, humans have adapted too. Near large lakes, people build ships and ports for easy travel on waterways. In places with flowing water, they build dams to control flooding. People drill wells in areas with little fresh water. The wells provide water for drinking and watering crops.

For thousands of years, humans have settled near water. Before cars and trains, boats were the best way to travel long distances. For example, fur traders traveled along rivers and lakes scattered around the Great Lakes of the United States and Canada. The traders received animal pelts from American Indians in exchange for things such as hats and blankets. Later, the rivers served as routes to float logs to other places. The logs provided lumber for early settlers to build homes. Today, people still use fresh water for transportation. The Great Lakes in North America provide connected water routes for shipping materials such as iron ore and coal.

FACT BOX
Canada is home to at least half the lakes on Earth! Lake Superior, on the U.S. and Canadian border, is the largest of these lakes. It holds about 3 quadrillion gallons (11 quadrillion liters) of water. That is more than the water of all the other Great Lakes combined.

ONTARIO

CANADA

Nipigon
Marathon
Thunder Bay
NNESOTA
Isle Royal
Michipicoten I.
Wawa
LAKE SUPERIOR
th
Keweenaw
Superior
Marquette
Sault Ste Marie

WISCONSIN
Escanaba
Manitoulin Island
Parry Sound
Door Peninsula
Alpena
Georgian Bay
Green Bay
LAKE HURON
Midland
Manitowoc
MICHIGAN
Owen Sound
Kingston

USA
Goderich
Oshawa
Toronto
LAKE ONTARIO
Milwaukee
Muskegon
Saginaw
Hamilton
Rochester
Racine
Holland
Sarnia
Buffalo
IOWA
Detroit
NEW YORK
Chicago
Windsor
Erie
LAKE ERIE
Gary
Toledo
Cleveland
ILLINOIS
INDIANA
Sandusky
Lorain
PENNSYLVANIA
OHIO

LAKE MICHIGAN

St. Lawrence

Although today people might choose a plane instead of a boat for travel, we still rely on water as a resource. We use fresh water as a source of food such as fish. We also enjoy lakes for fun activities such as swimming and water skiing.

13

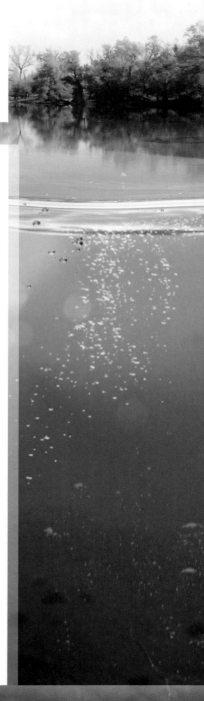

CHAPTER 3
BENEATH THE SURFACE

Beneath the surface, a lake swarms with activity. Many creatures live within the layers and zones of a lake. During warm months, the top layers of water are warm. The bottom layer is cold.

In a clear lake, sunlight can reach down about 30 feet (9 meters) or more. But sediment, algae, logs, or ice can block the sunlight. Organisms that need sunlight or require warmer water stay at the surface.

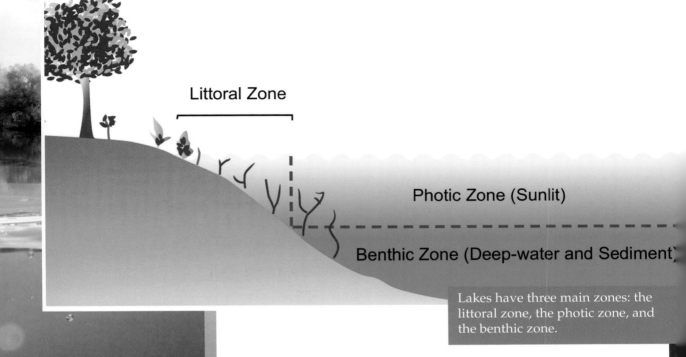

Littoral Zone

Photic Zone (Sunlit)

Benthic Zone (Deep-water and Sediment)

Lakes have three main zones: the littoral zone, the photic zone, and the benthic zone.

During winter, some lakes are covered in ice. Fish become sluggish and less active as temperatures decrease. Some plants go **dormant**. But sometimes the water temperature climbs or drops quickly. When this happens, fish and plants that have adapted to milder temperatures might not survive.

dormant—when breathing or other functions slow down for a period of time

RESERVOIRS

Some places have no lakes, so people create them! People build dams across rivers to hold back the water and create a lake. This kind of lake is called a **reservoir**. Reservoirs store water for later use such as watering crops. People also build dams on lakes to control water levels. Dams limit the amount of water that can flow from the lake. They can increase the water available for drinking and control floods. Some dams are used to provide electricity. As water flows through the dam to a river below, it spins a **turbine**, which produces power.

Humans aren't the only ones to build dams to create reservoirs. Beavers are very good at dam building. They gnaw on tree bark, eating the sugary layer underneath. Then they drag logs and branches through the water to build dams. Beavers seal the walls with mud and use stones for the base. These dams can hold back lots of water, just like dams built by people. Do you think early humans learned about dams and reservoirs from beavers?

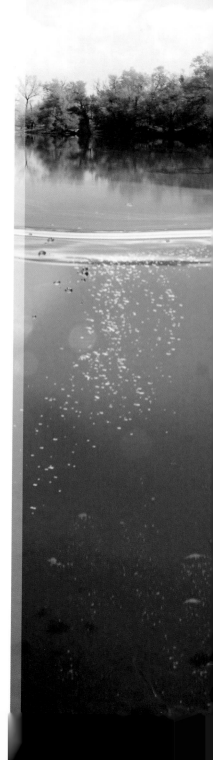

salmon in shallow water

FACT BOX

Some fish such as salmon need to move upstream during part of their life cycle. Dams can block this **migration**. In some places, fishways, which look a little like steps of water, are built around dams to help the fish get upstream.

migration—seasonal movement from one place to another
reservoir—an artificial lake used to store a large supply of water
turbine—an engine with blades that can be turned by a moving fluid such as steam or water

CHAPTER 4

GOING TO EXTREMES

Freshwater biome climates can differ, and not just in temperature. Some biomes receive as much as 80 inches (203 centimeters) of rainfall each year. Others get very little rain. Some places get mostly snow. Some are windy, while others are calm.

Earth's continents have a variety of climates.

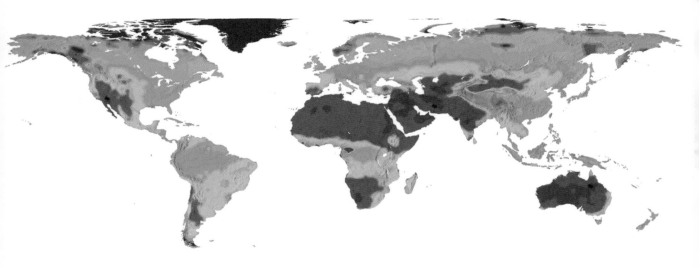

Global Temperatures

<0° 10° 20° 30° 40° 50° >60°

FROZEN WATER

Most of the fresh water on Earth's surface is frozen in glaciers and at the poles and not easily used. This is why freshwater biomes are so important. Even in freshwater areas, such as some lakes and rivers, the water freezes at times. But it is usually frozen only during the winter months.

People have learned to survive when these freshwater areas freeze. They drill holes into the ice to reach the water below. They even catch fish through these holes.

Fishermen drill holes through the ice to catch fish in the water below.

HOT WATER

Other freshwater biomes are hot. Hot springs, geysers, and mud pots form in clusters around the world. The clusters are near underground magma chambers. In the chambers, hot water or steam is trapped under a thin layer of Earth's surface. Channels connect it to the surface, just as a pipe carries water to a house.

The Grand Prismatic Spring in Yellowstone National Park can reach temperatures of about 189 degrees Fahrenheit (87 degrees Celsius).

People who live near hot water use it to heat their homes and bathwater and even produce electricity! The steam from the hot water spins turbines to produce electrical power.

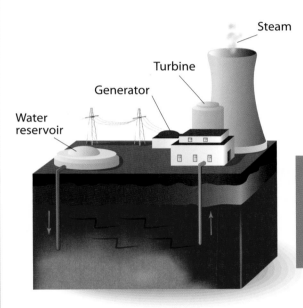

Geothermal power stations use heat from Earth's core to heat water. The heated water is cooled to create steam. The steam moves turbines that produce power.

HIDDEN WATER

People who don't live in a freshwater biome rely on groundwater. When water slowly trickles through the land surface, it's filtered through layers of sand and rock. This process helps clean the water. Groundwater is some of the best drinking water. People drill deep wells into the ground to find water for drinking and watering crops.

DISAPPEARING WATER

When an area doesn't receive rain for a long time, it's called a drought. They cause crops to fail and animals to die. Droughts can also lead to less food for people. Sometimes people waste water and make droughts worse.

One place where water is vanishing is on the prairie. Prairie potholes are shallow ponds. They form **habitats** for migrating birds and other animals. But many prairie potholes have been drained for farmland or buildings. People drain the water by digging ditches or burying pipes called tile in the prairie soil.

FACT BOX

Scientists estimate that the number of prairie potholes has decreased by as much as 90 percent in the United States and Canada over the last 125 years. This decrease leaves many animals at risk, including the endangered burrowing owl and the little brown bat.

prairie potholes

Some scientists think our use of coal and oil has warmed Earth. This warming affects how much it rains and snows. Warming temperatures can also melt ice caps and glaciers. In some areas, glaciers may melt completely and disappear. This is a growing problem. About 200 million people, mostly in the Andes and Himalayan Mountains, rely on glacier water for drinking.

habitat—the natural home or environment of an animal, plant, or other living thing

23

POLLUTION

Not all fresh water is usable. Some is trapped in glaciers. Some is polluted. And yet the demand for clean water is increasing because Earth's human population is increasing.

When we think about pollution, it's not just the garbage that you can see. Water can look clean but contain chemicals that are bad for people and animals.

NO SWIMMING

In the past people tended to settle near water sources. But as populations increase, people are moving to areas that don't have a lot of water. When towns are built in deserts, people there have to get water from deep wells for drinking, watering lawns, and bathing.

Just as humans affect the **quantity** of water, they can also change the **quality**. We use chemicals to make our lawns green, clean our clothes, and run our cars. These chemicals often make their way into our water. Many of these chemicals are bad for freshwater animal life. Chemicals can kill tadpoles or cause birds to lay eggs with thin shells, making it hard for chicks to survive.

FACT BOX
Scientists estimate that only 0.3 percent of Earth's water can be used by humans. The rest is too salty, polluted, frozen, or hard to reach.

quality—how good or bad something is
quantity—the amount or number of something

CHAPTER 5

OUR FRESHWATER FUTURE

Freshwater biomes are important to humans. We use fresh water to drink, to travel, to grow food, and to provide electricity. We also use fresh water for all sorts of fun activities—swimming, kayaking, or ice-skating. Although many freshwater biomes are disappearing or polluted, we can do things to fix the problem.

RAIN BARRELS

Rain barrels catch and store rainwater that flows off a roof. Rain barrels used to be common on farms and homes before modern tap water systems. Now they are popular again for conserving water. The rainwater can be used to water gardens and lawns. It saves water in the freshwater biome and reduces the use of water treated with chemicals.

FACT BOX
One inch (2.54 cm) of rainfall on a 1,000-square-foot (93-square-m) roof provides more than 600 gallons (2,271 liters) of storm water.

RAIN GARDENS

Rain gardens are pretty much just that! These gardens are planted with **native** plants. Rain gardens help rain soak into the ground. The plants and their roots keep the water from washing away with the soil. This reduces erosion and improves water quality. Rain gardens help to filter pollution and offer habitat for butterflies and other wildlife.

native—a plant or animal that is original to an area

BUFFERS

When you see tall grasses and plants along a lakeshore, it might seem messy. But these plants protect the water. It's actually healthier not to mow a yard all the way to the water's edge.

People can plant buffers, which are strips of tall grasses or native plants, along lakes, streams, and rivers. The buffers filter out soil and chemicals, helping protect water quality. Buffer plants have deeper roots than lawns, so they filter the groundwater as well.

CONSTRUCTED WETLANDS

Even though many wetlands have been drained, people can create new wetlands. Scientists design new wetlands to improve water quality. They plant areas of land similar to natural wetlands, which helps the land collect water. The wetland's plants and soils remove pollution from the water.

FACT BOX

What can you do? Rain gardens don't have to be huge. You can catch rainwater from your roof to water a planter. By keeping some storm water out of the sewers, you're helping the freshwater biome by saving water. Your mini rain garden will help filter water, reduce erosion, and might even provide a habitat for some bugs and worms.

CONVERTING SALT WATER

Many scientists are working on ways to purify salt water. For example, if you boil salt water in a pan and capture the steam, then you can let the steam turn back into fresh water. Large factories can do this with more water in a similar way, but it's expensive. This process can be used where drinking water is scarce.

By working together, we can keep our freshwater biomes healthy for ourselves and future generations.

Don Edwards San Francisco Bay National Wildlife Refuge in California

GLOSSARY

adapt (uh-DAPT)—to change in order to survive; a change in an animal or plant to better fit its environment is called an adaptation

algae (AL-jee)—a simple plant without stems, leaves, or roots

aquatic (uh-KWAH-tik)—having to do with water

current (KUHR-uhnt)—flowing water moving in one direction

dormant (DOR-muhnt)—when breathing or other functions slow down for a period of time

habitat (HAB-uh-tat)—the natural home or environment of an animal, plant, or other organism

migration (mye-GRAY-shuhn)—seasonal movement from one place to another

native (NAY-tuhv)—a plant or animal that is original to an area

nutrient (NOO-tree-uhnt)—a substance that provides nourishment needed for growth and survival

organism (OR-guh-niz-uhm)—a form of life, such as an animal, plant, or cell

photosynthesis (foh-toh-SIN-thuh-siss)—the process of using sunlight to make oxygen and food from carbon dioxide and water

quality (KWAHL-uh-tee)—how good or bad something is

quantity (KWAN-tuh-tee)—the amount or number of something

reservoir (REZ-ur-vwar)—an artificial lake used to store a large supply of water

saturated (SAH-chuh-rayt-uhd)—soaked with water

turbine (TUR-buhn)—an engine with blades that can be turned by a moving fluid such as steam or water

zooplankton (zoo-PLANGK-tuhn)—a small animal plankton in the water

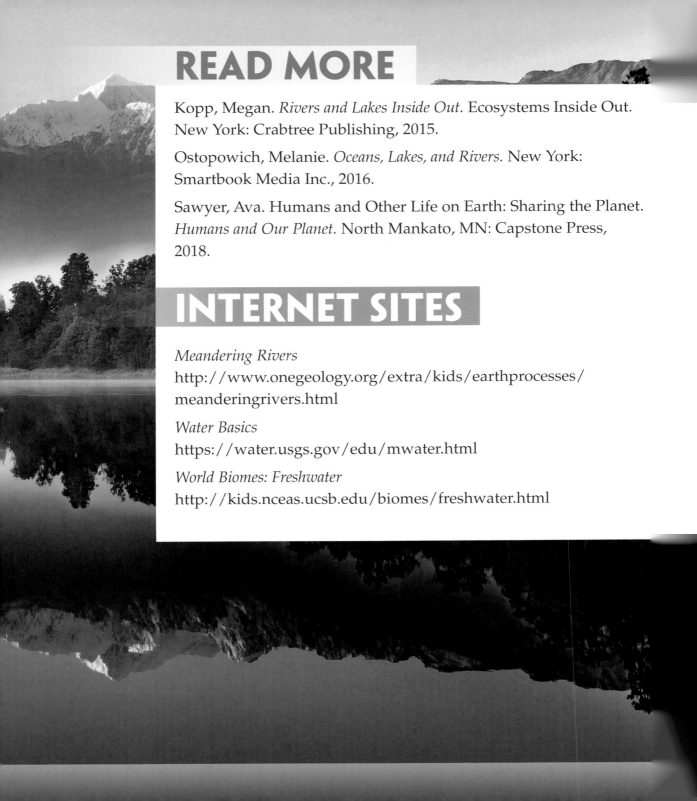

READ MORE

Kopp, Megan. *Rivers and Lakes Inside Out.* Ecosystems Inside Out. New York: Crabtree Publishing, 2015.

Ostopowich, Melanie. *Oceans, Lakes, and Rivers.* New York: Smartbook Media Inc., 2016.

Sawyer, Ava. Humans and Other Life on Earth: Sharing the Planet. *Humans and Our Planet.* North Mankato, MN: Capstone Press, 2018.

INTERNET SITES

Meandering Rivers
http://www.onegeology.org/extra/kids/earthprocesses/meanderingrivers.html

Water Basics
https://water.usgs.gov/edu/mwater.html

World Biomes: Freshwater
http://kids.nceas.ucsb.edu/biomes/freshwater.html

CRITICAL THINKING QUESTIONS

1. What are two ways humans can help preserve freshwater biomes?
2. Water flows more quickly when the land's slope is steep. What happens to the water's speed when the ground becomes flat?
3. Both freshwater crocodiles and saltwater crocodiles live on Earth. How do you think these two different species may have adapted to their biomes?

INDEX